52

POWERFUL

Success Strategies

TO IGNITE PRODUCTIVITY

Cathy Sexton

52 POWERFUL Success Strategies
TO IGNITE PRODUCTIVITY
Cathy Sexton
TPE Publishing

Published by TPE Publishing, Valley Park, MO
Copyright ©2015 Cathy Sexton
All rights reserved.

Copy editor: Linda Stroud, www.wordswithavoice.com

Cover and Interior Design: Davis Creative, www.DavisCreative.com

ISBN: 978-0-9966722-0-7

2015

To my husband Richard (my soul mate),
my daughter Tammy (the light of my life)
and all my angels in heaven!

Productivity isn't everything,
but it affects everything...

Productivity is a
measurement of the ROI
(return on investment)
of your Time, Money, & Energy"

- Cathy Sexton

Acknowledgments

As with most books, this would not be a reality without the help of others. My sincere gratitude goes to everyone who has touched my life.

To every family member, friend, client, associate, fellow business owner and even the villainous people I've encountered, without you, my life path would have been altered and this book may have taken a different path or no path at all.

To my dear friend and mentor, Lethia Owens, who suggested I reach out to my database on a regular basis with something short but valuable. With that challenge my "Action of the Week" was born.

To all the clients and contacts that respond weekly on how these tips, quotes and afformations hit the target or make their day and consistently encourage me to put them in a book.

To Noah St. John for sharing his knowledge and teachings of afformations. And to all the productivity experts who I have learned from or been influenced by.

To my audience that has tolerated my not-so-perfect writings of actions and tips over the years. To my editors Tammy Sexton, intern — Allis Yang and professional editor Linda Stroud for taking my weakness and making me look so good.

To my publishers Cathy and Jack Davis of Davis Creative for your encouragement, guidance, knowledge and friendship.

And to each and every person, acknowledged or not, who has had an impact on my life or upon my content and the direction of this book.

Contents

Foreword

Almost any professional would say it is their goal to become more productive, yet so many still struggle to effectively manage their time, energy and resources. Today's busy professional has to juggle increasing demands on their time, often leaving them feeling frustrated and overwhelmed.

I have to admit that this used to be me. I constantly sought better techniques and strategies to get more done and complete my work more efficiently. Yet each week it seemed I was falling more and more behind. I had tried all of the latest time management techniques but nothing seemed to work for me. If the new technique did work, it only worked for a little while. I was looking for a system and strategies I could implement and sustain the positive results.

My search for the prefect productivity tool ended when I realized two things:

1. There is NO perfect tool; and
2. My productivity is greatly enhanced when I understand and embrace my natural productivity style.

This was such a game changing revelation for me. This new insight has transformed how I live and work. Cathy's resources and coaching have helped to reduce my stress level and now I am able to get more done without working myself to death.

Cathy's book, *52 Powerful Productivity Tips*, is a fast, easy read and it offers practical ways to get organized, stay focused and leverage your resources to get more done. If you've ever wished for more hours in a day, I'm sorry to tell you it isn't going to happen. But this resource is the next best thing, because you'll quickly learn how to ignite your productivity and increase your profit.

Lethia Owens
President and CEO — Next Level Branding & Marketing
Ranked #8 Among the Top 30 Brand Gurus in the World

Introduction

Effective productivity isn't just a concept or an ideal, it's a necessary part of all of our lives today, and the degree to which we're able to be effective with our productive efforts can affect all aspects of our life. We each have only so many hours in a day and we each have to choose how we will use them. We marvel at the people who seem to have figured it out — those who have found the balance and manage to keep all the balls in the air. For most of us, however, there is a daily struggle with getting everything done and still having time for the ones we love and actually enjoying the fruits of our labor.

Many people these days are experiencing unprecedented levels of frustration and disillusionment with respect to their ability (or inability) to do it all and have it all. While we live in a world where doing it all and having it all is the stated goal, few of us are lucky enough or equipped to achieve that goal. Stress levels rise as the work pours in and we try to keep up, but find ourselves deeper and deeper in the hole even though we're stealing time from the rest we need and the ones we love to compensate for the overload at work.

This is not a healthy way to live. Over time, elevated stress levels can have a major impact on our relationships, our outlook on life and our health. And yet, we continue pushing forward thinking that surely something will magically change or we will gain control and be able to manage things better. Sometimes, we get so enmeshed in the day-to-day, we fail to recognize that there's even a problem with the way we're living as stress and non-productive behaviors become the norm. Recognizing and acknowledging that we're struggling with this unhealthy cycle is the first step to changing it. The second step is learning what to do differently and gathering the tools to help us do it.

I understand all too well the effects a never-ending workload, stress and ineffective productivity can have on a person's life and health. There was a time, not too long ago, when I was faced with a very serious decision regarding how I was living and managing my life. I stood at the same cross-road you may now be facing and had to choose: Would I continue on the destructive, unhealthy path I was on or would I make the necessary changes to improve my life and my health?

After being diagnosed with a stress-induced, life-threatening illness that could potentially leave my daughter motherless, my husband without a wife and me missing out on all the amazing milestones that go along with loving those two people, the path I needed to choose wasn't even a serious debate. But I also quickly realized that my life hadn't spiraled out of control because I made conscious choices to make it that way, but because I didn't know how to do things differently. The one thing I did know was that I wasn't in control of my life, my life was controlling me.

Once I recognized and acknowledged that the way I was managing my life was literally killing me and that I didn't know how to work differently, I set out to find the tools that would empower me to change. My personal journey of discovery led to what became my mission, my passion and my life's work. In my quest for answers, I came to understand the role organization, time management, procrastination and natural productivity styles play in our successful efforts (or failure) to effectively manage our lives. I also came to realize that I was not alone.

Knowing there are so many others out there who struggle with the same things I did is what drove me to put this book together. While I have spent years putting comprehensive programs together to help others climb out from under the weight of the demands in their lives, I felt there were some simple, straightforward concepts and tools that could be used by anyone wanting to make even the smallest changes. I used the acronym POWER-FUL to create the themes for each chapter and guide you through the reflections in the hope that taking the time to read, reflect on and implement each little tip will, in fact, make you more powerful and in control of your time, relationships and health.

I do want to mention the concept of afformations here too, since you will be seeing them throughout this book. It's not a misprint. Afformations are a valuable tool created by Noah St. John, one of the personal-growth mentors who led me to the answers I was seeking years ago. While affirmations are based on the belief that just saying something will make it so, afformations are based on the premise that if we ask ourselves empowering questions our mind will begin to focus on what we really want and stop focusing on what we don't want. Rather than trying to trick our minds into believing something that might not be true, with afformations we set our minds in motion to search for the answer and guide our path to making the positive things we want reality. If this is a new or unbelievable concept for you, just give it a try.

Doing it all and having it all may be the stated, highly sought-after goal, but it may not be best goal. I encourage you to consider the possibility that effectively managing what's on your proverbial plate and living a life that brings satisfaction in your work and personal life, not to mention enjoyment of both, would be a much better goal to have. That goal is attainable and my greatest hope is that the tips, quotes and afformations in this book will help and inspire you to reach it.

Here's to your productivity

Cathy

Productivity & Profit First Specialist

Chapter One

POWERFUL = Productivity Style: Working Authentically

Whether you are an entrepreneur, manager, administrative assistant or a seasoned professional running a division or an entire company, you have natural strengths and natural limitations. Too often we fall into work habits that go against our natural productivity style. This can cause frustration, stress, feelings of inadequacy or being overwhelmed and even total burnout.

Everything we accomplish, in business and in life, is based on two elements: How efficient and effective we are on a personal level and how successful we are at inspiring and motivating others.

Understanding your (and your team's) "Natural Productivity Style", through Productivity Style Assessment, will bring clarity in processing the work you do and provide you with best practices to become the best you can be.

By understanding and working within your "Productivity Style" you can:
- Increase your ability to achieve goals — more quickly and effectively
- Reduce stress and achieve optimal work/life balance
- Increase productivity, efficiency and effectiveness, while at the same time, improving your quality of life.

What's it worth to you to ***discover your Natural Productivity Style***, so you can maximize your results with less effort? This chapter will give you some tips to be more effective within your "Productivity Style".

Action:

Discover What Works

Everyone thinks, processes, reacts and works differently. There are many productivity styles out there, but the key is finding the ones that work for you. Some may work really well for some people, while others may not work at all. Try the tips in this book one by one. Discover what works for you and what doesn't. By eliminating tips that don't work and implementing those that do, you will be on your way to being truly productive. Remember it's not what you should do, it's what you will do that is important.

Quote:

"Thinking too long about doing something
is often the reason it never gets done."
~ Unknown

Afformation:

"Why is it so easy to find what works for me?"

How does this tip, quote or afformation relate to you and your productivity?

_____

_____

_____

_____

_____

_____

_____

_____

_____

_____

_____

What will you improve, change, STOP or start doing this week?

_____

_____

_____

_____

_____

_____

_____

_____

_____

_____

_____

_____

http://theproductivityexperts.com/52-powerful-success-strategies/powerful-results-form

Action:

Reflect on Your Productivity Work Style

Do you know your work style? When you know your work style, you can choose the processes that work best for you. You will get better results, faster, and with more enjoyment.

Ask yourself:
- How do I work best?
- What makes me feel committed to a task?
- What makes me follow through to the end?
- Do I need a quiet space or does music help?
- Do short or long spurts of time work best for me?
- When is my energy level at its highest?

Quote:

"Let us watch well our beginnings, and results will manage themselves."
~ Alexander Clark

Afformation:

"Why do I stay true to my personal work style?"

How does this tip, quote or afformation relate to you and your productivity?

_____

_____

_____

_____

_____

_____

_____

_____

_____

_____

_____

What will you improve, change, STOP or start doing this week?

_____

_____

_____

_____

_____

_____

_____

_____

_____

_____

_____

_____

_____

http://theproductivityexperts.com/52-powerful-success-strategies/powerful-results-form

Action:

Reduce Fatigue

Life seems to really keep us busy. The busyness and all that running around can often mean that you don't have time to get enough rest in your busy schedule. Lack of energy is one of the main causes of procrastination. Physical exhaustion and lack of sleep can lead to increased stress and anxiety, but, fortunately, the solution is simple. One of the best ways to reduce stress and anxiety is — you guessed it — getting enough rest.

Quote:

"In daily life, we must see that it is not happiness that makes us grateful, but gratefulness that makes us happy."
~ Brother David Steindl-Rast

Afformation:

"Why is it so easy to get needed rest?"

How does this tip, quote or afformation relate to you and your productivity?

_____

_____

_____

_____

_____

_____

_____

_____

_____

_____

_____

What will you improve, change, STOP or start doing this week?

_____

_____

_____

_____

_____

_____

_____

_____

_____

_____

_____

_____

http://theproductivityexperts.com/52-powerful-success-strategies/powerful-results-form

Action:

Be Decisive and Move On

Every minute spent on being indecisive slows down your ability to take action and keeps you from accomplishing more. For example, rather than spending four hours researching travel airfares only to save $20, give yourself 30 - 45 minutes to compare prices and make a decision. Your time is worth more in the long run.

Quote:

"Never let yesterday use up today."
~ Richard H. Nelson

Afformation:

"Why is it so easy to be decisive?

How does this tip, quote or afformation relate to you and your productivity?

_____
_____
_____
_____
_____
_____
_____
_____
_____
_____
_____

What will you improve, change, STOP or start doing this week?

_____
_____
_____
_____
_____
_____
_____
_____
_____
_____
_____

http://theproductivityexperts.com/52-powerful-success-strategies/powerful-results-form

Action:

Recognize How Work Styles Affect You

There are some common work styles that greatly affect your ability to be productive. Take a moment and recognize which of these styles might apply to you, or those you work with, and how particular styles may be hindering your productivity. Most importantly, honestly consider which of these styles could be causing you to be the one doing the hindering?

Socializer: Wastes incredible amounts of time on frivolous conversations.

Emailer: Never uses the phone and each email is a chapter in a book.

Alarmist: OMG! They are the creator of crisis. No matter how small... it's big.

Meetingizer: Obsessed with talking about what needs to be done, with nothing accomplished but another meeting.

Procrastinator: It never fails, they always need it now! And for some reason, their emergencies are now yours.

Quote:

*"I have a lot of faults. I often interrupt in meetings.
I talk too loud. I talk too fast"*
~ Aaron Levie

Afformation:

"Why am I so good at not hindering others productivity?"

How does this tip, quote or afformation relate to you and your productivity?

_____

_____

_____

_____

_____

_____

_____

_____

_____

_____

_____

What will you improve, change, STOP or start doing this week?

_____

_____

_____

_____

_____

_____

_____

_____

_____

_____

_____

_____

http://theproductivityexperts.com/52-powerful-success-strategies/powerful-results-form

Action:

Consider Whether Music Would Help Your Productivity

Music can increase your productivity depending on your work style. For some, music can be a way to increase focus. For others, music may make it difficult to concentrate. Music may also increase or decrease workplace productivity overall, depending on the type of music. Try sampling different types of music to see if one type or another helps your productivity. If you work in an office setting, it's best to use headphones so as not to disturb others.

Quote:

"Music can change the world because it can change people."
~ Bono

Afformation:

"Why does using music help my focus so well?"

How does this tip, quote or afformation relate to you and your productivity?

_____

_____

_____

_____

_____

_____

_____

_____

_____

_____

_____

What will you improve, change, STOP or start doing this week?

_____

_____

_____

_____

_____

_____

_____

_____

_____

_____

_____

_____

http://theproductivityexperts.com/52-powerful-success-strategies/powerful-results-form

Other Resources:

What's your productivity challenge?
https://app.hatchbuck.com/OnlineForm/50165738227

Productivity self-assessment:
http://theproductivityexperts.com/self-assessment

Productivity store
http://theproductivityexperts.com/shop/

For More Weekly Actions
http://theproductivityexperts.com/tips/

25 Productivity Strategies to get more done eBook
http://theproductivityexperts.com/ebook-bonus

Productivity Blog
http://theproductivityexperts.com/blog/

Check out Cathy Sexton's speaking schedule
http://theproductivityexperts.com/productivity-speaker/
cathys-calendar/

Chapter Two

POWERFUL = Organization: Clutter and Space

When it comes to getting organized, we're our own worst enemies. We keep stuff, which turns into clutter, because we convince ourselves we'll need these items — even if we haven't us`ed them in five years and don't quite know where we've put them. There seems to be a security factor in just knowing they're around... somewhere.

But then we can't seem to find them when we need them. What most of us really need is a personal push to get organized — understanding how to separate ourselves emotionally from the possessions we no longer need and that clutter our minds as well as our space.

Organization is key to being able to properly manage your time. If you are unorganized, you are likely to waste a large amount of time. For example, in the workplace you can waste time by searching for lost or misplaced documents. The same can be said for the home; if you are unorganized, you can spend hours searching for your glasses or car keys.

Clutter comes in many forms: physical, digital, mental, financial, and social.

A lot of our time that we consider lost is really taken up by our clutter. Think about all of the clutter we have to care for, clean up, organize, and keep up with.

Reduce your stress by reducing your clutter and spend the time you gain on something you love.

Action:

Stay With It — It's Not an Event, It's a Process

Do you find yourself in a cycle of feeling suddenly inspired to get organized, cleaning up the clutter and then feeling frustrated when the mess has — once again — accumulated in a week or two? After we organize, it may seem like the organized area will stay that way. However, day-by-day, the organization will slowly become disorganized right before your eyes. Look for opportunities to organize your space every day. Taking just a few minutes in a day will make everything easier in the long run.

Quote:

"Clutter is nothing more than postponed decisions."
~ Barbara Hemphill

Afformation:

"Why do I stay so organized?"

How does this tip, quote or afformation relate to you and your productivity?

_____

_____

_____

_____

_____

_____

_____

_____

_____

_____

_____

What will you improve, change, STOP or start doing this week?

_____

_____

_____

_____

_____

_____

_____

_____

_____

_____

_____

_____

_____

http://theproductivityexperts.com/52-powerful-success-strategies/powerful-results-form

Action:

Use The 5 D's of Decisions

There are only five decisions you need to make about any piece of paper:

Can I_____?

- Delete it? — Toss, shred, and discard.
- Delegate? — Is this the best use of my time? If not, delegate it.
- Do it now? — Can it be done in 2 minutes or less? Just do it!
- Defer for filing? (Reference) — Papers you may never need, but are afraid to throw away. (Did you know that 80% of the papers we file, we never look at a second time? Have you thought about going paperless?)
- Define the action? Ask:
  - When is it due?
  - How long will it take?
  - Who else is involved?
  - When should I schedule it.

Quote:

"I always thought my friend was disorganized, but after helping her move, I stand corrected. The label on a box I carried read 'Stuff off the floor.'"
~ Ting Sun, Monument, Colorado

Afformation:

"Why do I always use the 5 D's effectively?"

How does this tip, quote or afformation relate to you and your productivity?

_____

_____

_____

_____

_____

_____

_____

_____

_____

_____

_____

_____

What will you improve, change, STOP or start doing this week?

_____

_____

_____

_____

_____

_____

_____

_____

_____

_____

_____

_____

_____

_____

http://theproductivityexperts.com/52-powerful-success-strategies/powerful-results-form

Action:

Organize Your To-Do List

When compiling your To-Do list, consider color coding your tasks or numbering them in order of priority. Don't be afraid to assign or delegate some of the tasks to others if you need the extra help.

- Be sure to assign due dates and estimate the time needed to complete each task.
- Prioritizing is key to To-Do list success.
- Have a master list for everything. Break this down to <u>this week</u>, <u>this month</u>, <u>this quarter</u> and <u>someday</u>.
- Review this week's list and only put a maximum of 5 items on your list for today. (If you finish, you can always go back to your master list and get more.)

Quote:

"Vision without action is just a dream. Action without vision just passes the time. Vision with action can change the world."
~ Loren Eiseley

Afformation:

"Why is my to-do list always prioritized and workable?"

How does this tip, quote or affirmation relate to you and your productivity?

_____

_____

_____

_____

_____

_____

_____

_____

_____

_____

What will you improve, change, STOP or start doing this week?

_____

_____

_____

_____

_____

_____

_____

_____

_____

_____

_____

http://theproductivityexperts.com/52-powerful-success-strategies/powerful-results-form

Action:

Create a Better Filing System

Consider using "straight tab" filing, so the tab position for all hanging folders lines up one behind the other. It is much easier on the eyes than staggering the tabs left, middle, and right. Also, always put the tabs on the front of the file folder. This way, you pull the tab and the file opens for you.

- Mark labels clearly: Use a dark marker, label maker, or computer labeling system
- Eliminate the small plastic tabs on your hanging folders. Great replacements for small plastic tabs:
  - Fast Tabs = Tab attached gives large area for labels
  - Avery® 5567 Hanging File Tabs
  - Smead Viewables.™

Quote:

"To think too long about doing a thing often becomes its undoing."
~ Eva Young

Afformation:

"Why can I always find what I am looking for in my files?"

How does this tip, quote or afformation relate to you and your productivity?

_____

_____

_____

_____

_____

_____

_____

_____

_____

_____

_____

What will you improve, change, STOP or start doing this week?

_____

_____

_____

_____

_____

_____

_____

_____

_____

_____

_____

_____

_____

http://theproductivityexperts.com/52-powerful-success-strategies/powerful-results-form

Action:

Address Common Filing Mistakes

One mistake that is often made in filing papers, emails, or electronic files: Filing items you don't need to file. Did you know that 80% of the papers we file we never look at a second time? Before filing ask yourself:
- Do I really need to keep this?
- Do I use it often?
- Do I need this for legal or tax reasons?
- How easily can I find this information elsewhere?
- What's the worst thing that will happen if I don't have it? (If you can live with that answer, you can probably get rid of it.)

Quote:

"Taking some time to think about what and why we are keeping certain files will enhance finding what you need when you need it. Note: 80% of what we file, we never look at a second time!
"Never let yesterday use up today."
~ Richard H. Nelson

Afformation:

"Why is it so easy to keep my filing up to date?"

How does this tip, quote or afformation relate to you and your productivity?

_____

_____

_____

_____

_____

_____

_____

_____

_____

_____

_____

What will you improve, change, STOP or start doing this week?

_____

_____

_____

_____

_____

_____

_____

_____

_____

_____

_____

_____

http://theproductivityexperts.com/52-powerful-success-strategies/powerful-results-form

Action:

Clear Space

Do you ever find yourself looking around for the same thing over and over? Do you have a cluttered work area? Start off by clearing away papers and things that aren't needed. Have a place for everything and everything will be in its place. Having a proper place for everything means that you have an organized work area, which makes you more productive. Make these places easy to reach and find. Having a proper place for everything is a big step in reaching your productivity goals.

When you're done for the day, take a bit of time to tidy up your workspace. Do what you can to improve the cleanliness and order of your area, so that you can come in the next day to a neat and uncluttered space. This allows you to have a fresh start without the leftovers from days gone by. Clear Space = Clear Mind. It's worth the time.

Quote:

"Being organized leaves more room for spontaneity."
~ Kimberley Pappas

Afformation:

"Why is it so easy to keep my desk uncluttered?"

How does this tip, quote or afformation relate to you and your productivity?

_____

_____

_____

_____

_____

_____

_____

_____

_____

_____

What will you improve, change, STOP or start doing this week?

_____

_____

_____

_____

_____

_____

_____

_____

_____

_____

_____

_____

http://theproductivityexperts.com/52-powerful-success-strategies/powerful-results-form

Action:

Take Control

Eliminate clutter. If you put it away when you're finished you won't have to deal with it a second, third or fourth time.

Today's mail becomes tomorrow's pile, so make decisions daily. Unaddressed piles turn into chaos.

I have been asked many times, "Are some people incapable of being organized?" Answer: No, it just takes some people longer to find what works for them and learn the process. If you believe you can't be organized, the bottom line is you just don't want to be or aren't willing to make organization a priority.

The more organized you are, the easier it will be to deal with last minute and unexpected problems.

Quote:

"Waiting is a trap. There will always be reasons to wait... The truth is, there are only two things in life, reasons and results, and reasons simply don't count."
~ Robert Anthony

Afformation:

"Why am I so good at being and staying organized?"

How does this tip, quote or afformation relate to you and your productivity?

_____
_____
_____
_____
_____
_____
_____
_____
_____
_____

What will you improve, change, STOP or start doing this week?

_____
_____
_____
_____
_____
_____
_____
_____
_____
_____
_____
_____

http://theproductivityexperts.com/52-powerful-success-strategies/powerful-results-form

Action:

Create the Appearance of Order Quickly

When things are helter-skelter, you feel out of control. It's important to first create the appearance of order and clear some space to work.

- **Gather:** Stack everything in one neat pile. Don't worry about sorting or prioritizing. For now, just create some room; take a breath and a moment to enjoy the clear surface in front of you. Notice the space you have to work with. Great time to dust!
- **Filter/Sort:** Discard what can be trashed/shredded etc., then create 3 piles:
  - Delegate pile — Keep a sticky note handy to jot down what needs to be done. Distribute later.
  - Filing pile — Set to the side, not on your desk.
  - Action pile — Determine:
    - Due date?
    - How long will it take to do it?
    - Who needs to be involved?
- **Prioritize Action Pile & Get Started**

Quote:

"Kind words can be short and easy to speak, but their echoes are truly endless."
~ Mother Teresa

Afformation:

"Why is it so easy to keep a clean and organized desk?"

How does this tip, quote or afformation relate to you and your productivity?

_____
_____
_____
_____
_____
_____
_____
_____
_____
_____
_____

What will you improve, change, STOP or start doing this week?

_____
_____
_____
_____
_____
_____
_____
_____
_____
_____
_____
_____

http://theproductivityexperts.com/52-powerful-success-strategies/powerful-results-form

Other Resources:

What's your productivity challenge?
https://app.hatchbuck.com/OnlineForm/50165738227

Productivity self-assessment:
http://theproductivityexperts.com/self-assessment

Productivity store
http://theproductivityexperts.com/shop/

For More Weekly Actions
http://theproductivityexperts.com/tips/

25 Productivity Strategies to get more done eBook
http://theproductivityexperts.com/ebook-bonus

Productivity Blog
http://theproductivityexperts.com/blog/

Check out Cathy Sexton's speaking schedule
http://theproductivityexperts.com/productivity-speaker/
cathys-calendar/

Chapter Three

POWERFUL = Willingness to Do It Differently: Mindset and Habits

"Insanity is doing the same thing over and over again but expecting different results." ~ Albert Einstein.

I have heard this quote many times in many different ways. No matter how it's stated, it has a profound effect on our mindset, habits and, of course, our productivity.

We all have some habits — really more than we think. If asked, we can generally think of a couple of bad personal habits, but few of us are aware of our "work" habits. Unfortunately, a lot of our work habits are related to our young adult years, college and first job experiences. These habits can be good or bad. It is important to be more aware of how our habits fit into our changing lives, technology, environment, co-worker relationships, current job duties and company expectations. In today's business environment you are expected to be able to manage the constant changes, meet the needs of increased productivity, complexity, volume of work and information regarding your job.

Changing habits might help our productivity, but if we don't change the mindset it's almost impossible to change the habit long term. Mindset change is based on recognizing that you have a choice. How you interpret your situation is really in your control. You can interpret situations with a fixed mindset or with a growth mindset. So when you face a habit, challenge or setback that you want to change, identify your fixed mindset and challenge it with a growth mindset. Then take action with the growth mindset.

Action:

Create a Toolkit to Help You Achieve Balance

Take a moment and think about what balance means for you. Create a tool-kit that will help you achieve that balance.

Find fixes to bring you back to your centered state. These days, we're stretched in so many directions at such a fast pace it's easy to feel tired. When you're frenzied, take time to stop. Find some moments every day to focus only on you and take time to rest.

It might be carrying pictures of your kids to look at when you feel stressed, taking a moment to sit in a quiet room and drink an herbal tea, or meditat-ing for a few minutes every day at the office. Even a little "Take 5" can help. Take 5 breaths, hold each one for 5 seconds, then blow out for 5 seconds... ahhhh feel the relief.

Quote:

"The Old Year has gone. Let the dead past bury its own dead. The New Year has taken possession of the clock of time. All hail the duties and pos-sibilities of the coming twelve months!"
~ Edward Payson Powell

Afformation:

"Why do I have and use a toolkit that helps me create balance?"

How does this tip, quote or afformation relate to you and your productivity?

_____

_____

_____

_____

_____

_____

_____

_____

_____

_____

What will you improve, change, STOP or start doing this week?

_____

_____

_____

_____

_____

_____

_____

_____

_____

_____

_____

_____

_____

http://theproductivityexperts.com/52-powerful-success-strategies/powerful-results-form

Action:

Deal With Recurring Habits

If you find yourself backsliding into old behaviors, be GLAD!

When you recognize a recurring behavior, you can change it. Recommit to your GOAL and go back to trying and recommitting to the new behavior. Before you know it, it will become a subconscious habit. Two steps forward and one step back will still get you where you want to go.

Quote:

"It's never too late to be what you have been."
~ George Eliot

Afformation:

"Why is it so easy to create new habits?"

How does this tip, quote or afformation relate to you and your productivity?

_____

_____

_____

_____

_____

_____

_____

_____

_____

_____

_____

What will you improve, change, STOP or start doing this week?

_____

_____

_____

_____

_____

_____

_____

_____

_____

_____

_____

_____

_____

http://theproductivityexperts.com/52-powerful-success-strategies/powerful-results-form

Action:

Change Your Work Habits

Feel like you don't have enough hours in the day?

Your work day is supposed to finish at 4 p.m., but for some reason, you never seem to make it out of the office until 6 or 7 p.m.

Review possible reasons for staying late:
- Colleagues are working late, so you feel obligated to do the same.
- You've spent much of your day handling others' requests.

It's time to re-tool your work habits. Make a commitment to start leaving work on time. Plan your day and tasks based on your new time schedule. You will not only get more done during the day, you will also have more time at the end of your day for family and friends.

Quote:

"Parkinson's Law — Work expands to fill the time available for its completion."

Afformation:

"Why is it so easy to tweak my work habits?"

How does this tip, quote or afformation relate to you and your productivity?

_____

_____

_____

_____

_____

_____

_____

_____

_____

_____

What will you improve, change, STOP or start doing this week?

_____

_____

_____

_____

_____

_____

_____

_____

_____

_____

_____

_____

http://theproductivityexperts.com/52-powerful-success-strategies/powerful-results-form

Action:

Do More, Save More

Handle things at once. When it comes to email, voicemail, or paperwork, set aside time to work on these items. Take action when you do work on them, so that you don't have to come back to it later. The accumulated time that you save can actually add up to around 10 hours per month.

Quote:

"Don't say you don't have enough time. You have exactly the same number of hours per day that were given to Helen Keller, Pasteur, Michelangelo, Mother Teresa, Leonardo da Vinci, Thomas Jefferson, and Albert Einstein."
~ H. Jackson Brown

Afformation:

"Why do I choose to do things now rather than later?"

How does this tip, quote or afformation relate to you and your productivity?

_____

_____

_____

_____

_____

_____

_____

_____

_____

_____

What will you improve, change, STOP or start doing this week?

_____

_____

_____

_____

_____

_____

_____

_____

_____

_____

_____

http://theproductivityexperts.com/52-powerful-success-strategies/powerful-results-form

Action:

Redefine Perfection

Is "perfect" your end goal? Instead of thinking "perfect," consider:
- "Done" is better than "perfect."
- "Useful" is better than "perfect."
- "Mastery" is better than "perfect."

There will always be a sense that something can be improved. Striving for perfection, then, is a less productive goal than striving for more specific goals related to completing tasks.

Quote:

"To improve is to change; to be perfect is to change often."
~ Winston Churchill

Afformation:

"Why do I choose to rethink perfection?"

How does this tip, quote or afformation relate to you and your productivity?

_____

_____

_____

_____

_____

_____

_____

_____

_____

_____

What will you improve, change, STOP or start doing this week?

_____

_____

_____

_____

_____

_____

_____

_____

_____

_____

_____

_____

http://theproductivityexperts.com/52-powerful-success-strategies/powerful-results-form

Other Resources:

What's your productivity challenge?
https://app.hatchbuck.com/OnlineForm/50165738227

Productivity self-assessment:
http://theproductivityexperts.com/self-assessment

Productivity store
http://theproductivityexperts.com/shop/

For More Weekly Actions
http://theproductivityexperts.com/tips/

25 Productivity Strategies to get more done eBook
http://theproductivityexperts.com/ebook-bonus

Productivity Blog
http://theproductivityexperts.com/blog/

Check out Cathy Sexton's speaking schedule
http://theproductivityexperts.com/productivity-speaker/
cathys-calendar/

Chapter Four

POWERFUL = Email Overload: Processes and Outlook

In today's world, we can describe email as both an indispensable tool and productivity drain. It's happened to the best of us; although you rely on email to communicate, the number of messages coming through your inbox each day can drain hours of productivity.

Sure, you could just stay logged out for a while. But when you go a few days without checking your email, suddenly you're up to your neck in unread emails. Which emails are important? Which should you read first? All of these concerns can lead to you becoming stressed out and have a negative effect on your productivity.

In a time when the average business user spends more than **20% of their day processing email**, the question seems to be, "How can I get through my emails faster?" Email is like doing laundry: it seems to be a never-ending task with no end in sight.

You can learn how to get through email faster. Fast is good, but it's not the only thing that makes a difference. Eventually, no matter who you are and how fast you are at processing email, the volume of messages coming in will exceed the number that you can process. ***The key is how you process, receive, and, most importantly, how you choose to use your time.***

Action:

Get Better Responses From Your Emails

Use categories before your subject — (think verbs). This way, the receiver knows what action needs to happen. You can give more details in the body, but the subject line tells the story.

- **Action:**   re: Action: Meeting 5-12 @ 1PM — Main Conference Room
- **Delivery:** re: Delivery: Action list for new floor layout
- **Confirm:** re: Confirm: Lunch today at 11:30 @ Brio
- **Info:**   re: Info: FYI vacation schedule
- **Request:** re: Request: All budgets turned in by 5pm Friday

Quote:

"The difference between a successful person and others is not a lack of strength, not a lack of knowledge, but rather in a lack of will."
~ Vince Lombardi

Afformation

"Why do I get such great responses from my emails?"

How does this tip, quote or afformation relate to you and your productivity?

_____

_____

_____

_____

_____

_____

_____

_____

_____

_____

_____

What will you improve, change, STOP or start doing this week?

_____

_____

_____

_____

_____

_____

_____

_____

_____

_____

_____

_____

http://theproductivityexperts.com/52-powerful-success-strategies/powerful-results-form

Action:

Use B-A-B to Communicate Better Emails

B — Use bullet points or numbered lists whenever possible

A — Action up front, save the details for later

B — Be brief, keep it short and simple with one topic per email —
Stay on topic.

Also, ask yourself, "Is this the best way of communicating, or should I use the phone, speak in person, or wait for a meeting?" Think about the receiver, *not* the sender.

Quote:

"E-mail, instant messaging, and cell phones give us fabulous communication ability, but because we live and work in our own little worlds, that communication is totally disorganized."
~ Marilyn vos Savant

Afformation:

"Why am I so good at using the B-A-B email process?"

How does this tip, quote or afformation relate to you and your productivity?

_____

_____

_____

_____

_____

_____

_____

_____

_____

_____

_____

What will you improve, change, STOP or start doing this week?

_____

_____

_____

_____

_____

_____

_____

_____

_____

_____

_____

_____

http://theproductivityexperts.com/52-powerful-success-strategies/powerful-results-form

Action:

Adopt the 24-Hour Rule

From time to time, you will be tempted to send a not-so-nice response to someone. You may even have every right to be upset with them.

My suggestion is to write an email in draft form with no addressed recipient. Then, wait 24 hours before sending. If you wait that 24 hours before hitting "send", you'll find that, 90% of the time, you will have calmed down and realized that the email might not be the best solution. Give yourself time to process your thoughts and feelings and either rewrite the email or decide to have a personal conversation in order to clear up the matter.

Quote:

"I don't believe in e-mail. I'm an old-fashioned girl. I prefer calling and hanging up." ~ Sarah Jessica Parker

Afformation:

"Why do I always take 24 hours before sending an email when I am upset?"

How does this tip, quote or afformation relate to you and your productivity?

_____

_____

_____

_____

_____

_____

_____

_____

_____

_____

What will you improve, change, STOP or start doing this week?

_____

_____

_____

_____

_____

_____

_____

_____

_____

_____

_____

http://theproductivityexperts.com/52-powerful-success-strategies/powerful-results-form

Action:

Keep Email Niceties Brief

While it is fine to offer a warm greeting at the outset of your email, it can also become distracting if it's too long. Individuals don't have much time and don't want to read emails. They scan them, so make sure you put your action needed up front. Then, place niceties, chitchat, or other background information at the end of your email so your message is not lost in the middle.

Quote:

"A five-minute call replaces the time it takes to read and reply to the original email and read and reply to their reply... or replies. And I no longer spend 20+ minutes crafting the perfect email — no need to."
~ Simon Sinek

Afformation:

"Why am I so good at sending brief but concise emails?"

How does this tip, quote or afformation relate to you and your productivity?

_____

_____

_____

_____

_____

_____

_____

_____

_____

_____

_____

What will you improve, change, STOP or start doing this week?

_____

_____

_____

_____

_____

_____

_____

_____

_____

_____

_____

_____

_____

http://theproductivityexperts.com/52-powerful-success-strategies/powerful-results-form

Action:

Process Your Email Daily

Stop checking, reviewing, or reading the same email multiple times without acting.

Schedule 2 or 3 times a day to process your email.

Do not use your inbox as a storage unit; once you have read an email, take some kind of action on it.

When reading email, make a decision at that moment.
- Trash — discard
- Forward — redirect
- Just Do It — something easy to handle with no further action — get it done and over with.
- Drag and file
- Action needed — Flag, drag to create task, put on your to-do list and schedule time to work on it.

Quote:

"As we let our own light shine, we unconsciously give other people permission to do the same."
~ Nelson Mandela

Afformation:

"Why is it so easy to deal with my email?"

How does this tip, quote or afformation relate to you and your productivity?

_____

_____

_____

_____

_____

_____

_____

_____

_____

_____

What will you improve, change, STOP or start doing this week?

_____

_____

_____

_____

_____

_____

_____

_____

_____

_____

_____

_____

_____

http://theproductivityexperts.com/52-powerful-success-strategies/powerful-results-form

Action:

Use This Outlook Tasks Tip

Are you using Outlook tasks?

If you use the tasks list, you probably don't need to see your completed tasks. You only need to see what lies ahead. It's easy to hide completed tasks: Go to "View," "Current View," and select "Active Tasks." If you're not using Outlook tasks, you might want to consider utilizing your Outlook more effectively.

Quote:

"Time is a great healer, but a poor beautician."
~ Lucille S. Harper

Afformation:

"Why am I so productive today?"

How does this tip, quote or afformation relate to you and your productivity?

_____

_____

_____

_____

_____

_____

_____

_____

_____

_____

What will you improve, change, STOP or start doing this week?

_____

_____

_____

_____

_____

_____

_____

_____

_____

_____

_____

_____

http://theproductivityexperts.com/52-powerful-success-strategies/powerful-results-form

Other Resources:

What's your productivity challenge?
https://app.hatchbuck.com/OnlineForm/50165738227

Productivity self-assessment:
http://theproductivityexperts.com/self-assessment

Productivity store
http://theproductivityexperts.com/shop/

For More Weekly Actions
http://theproductivityexperts.com/tips/

25 Productivity Strategies to get more done eBook
http://theproductivityexperts.com/ebook-bonus

Productivity Blog
http://theproductivityexperts.com/blog/

Check out Cathy Sexton's speaking schedule
http://theproductivityexperts.com/productivity-speaker/
cathys-calendar/

Chapter Five

POWERFUL = **R**educe Procrastination

How do I put things off? That would be a long list for most of us. You can only truly do one thing at a time, so procrastination can occur when we have to choose one task over the other. It's when we repeatedly procrastinate on the same task over and over, or beyond its due date, that causes problems.

So what causes procrastination? Laziness, no will power, or lack of time management skills are typically blamed and, yes, these can be the cause, but most likely not. Procrastination that causes us to miss deadlines or put off a dreaded task is based on a powerful mindset that "short-term pleasure or relief is better than long-term results." The procrastinator may also fail to engage a positive action for reasons such as: distraction, misguided beliefs, or incompetency. But there are other possible explanations including, but not limited to:

- Fear
- Lack of Energy
- Perfectionism
- Difficulty of task
- Lack of motivation
- Rebellion
- Mental block
- Lack of confidence
- Project too large

- Length of time
- Someone else's goals
- Arrogance
- Bad habits
- Stress
- Disorganization
- Lack of time-management skills
- Etc.

Procrastination, the habit of putting tasks off to the last possible minute, can be a major problem in both your personal and professional life. Consequences of procrastination include: missed opportunities, stress, feeling overwhelmed, resentment, over working and guilt. Don't let procrastination rule your life.

Action:

Make a List and Check It Twice

Santa isn't the only one who should be making a list and checking it twice. Write down your wish list of *things you'd like to accomplish*, and be ruthless about whittling it down to the *things you must do*. Wouldn't it be great to make handmade gifts and give out cookies baked from scratch to friends, family, your child's teachers, and the mailman? Sure. Is it realistic for you to try to do that and still be able to do other things, like sleep? Only you can decide for yourself what you're willing to commit to and what you can *realistically* commit to. After your list is whittled down, set a plan of action. When will I do this? How long will it take me? Who could I delegate to? Who do I need to help me accomplish this?

Quote:

"Maybe Christmas, the Grinch thought, doesn't come from a store."
~ Dr. Seuss

Afformation:

"Why do I always enjoy my holiday and don't push myself over the edge?"

How does this tip, quote or afformation relate to you and your productivity?

_____

_____

_____

_____

_____

_____

_____

_____

_____

_____

_____

What will you improve, change, STOP or start doing this week?

_____

_____

_____

_____

_____

_____

_____

_____

_____

_____

_____

_____

http://theproductivityexperts.com/52-powerful-success-strategies/powerful-results-form

Action:

Outsmart Procrastination With a Quick Inner Dialogue

ACTION STEPS — Pin down the problem task with these 5 questions:
- What am I waiting for?
- When is a good time to do it?
- How will I know it's the right time?
- When will I start?
- What's the first step?

Quote:

"There are people who put their dreams in a little box and say, 'Yes, I've got dreams, of course I've got dreams.' Then they put the box away and bring it out once in awhile to look in it, and yep, they're still there."
~ Unknown

Afformation:

"Why is it so easy to tackle procrastination?"

How does this tip, quote or afformation relate to you and your productivity?

_____
_____
_____
_____
_____
_____
_____
_____
_____
_____
_____

What will you improve, change, STOP or start doing this week?

_____
_____
_____
_____
_____
_____
_____
_____
_____
_____
_____
_____
_____

http://theproductivityexperts.com/52-powerful-success-strategies/powerful-results-form

Action:

Reduce Procrastination Through Delegation

Procrastination isn't a result of laziness or a lack of resolve. It generally involves fear of failure, dislike, or a natural result of overload. Maybe it's time to involve others. Consider asking for help.

- Find an accountability partner
- Delegate
- Barter
- Don't be afraid to ask others for their help!

Quote:

"Help others get ahead. You will always stand taller with someone else on your shoulders."
~ Bob Moawad

Afformation:

"Why do I choose to delegate in order to reduce procrastination?"

How does this tip, quote or afformation relate to you and your productivity?

_____

_____

_____

_____

_____

_____

_____

_____

_____

_____

_____

What will you improve, change, STOP or start doing this week?

_____

_____

_____

_____

_____

_____

_____

_____

_____

_____

_____

_____

_____

http://theproductivityexperts.com/52-powerful-success-strategies/powerful-results-form

Action:

Set the Scene

Procrastination is perhaps the number-one enemy of your productivity. When you put things off, the amount of work you eventually have to do just builds up, leading to poor efficiency of projects. Your chances for making a mistake spikes due to rushing. Set the scene:

- Work with a clean desk — reduces distractions and helps focus
- Reduce projects to bite-size tasks
- Plan around possible interruptions
- Assign deadlines
- Block off time on your calendar

Quote:

"A year from now you may wish you had started today."
~ Karen Lamb

Afformation:

Why do I set the scene successfully to avoid procrastination?

How does this tip, quote or afformation relate to you and your productivity?

_____
_____
_____
_____
_____
_____
_____
_____
_____
_____
_____

What will you improve, change, STOP or start doing this week?

_____
_____
_____
_____
_____
_____
_____
_____
_____
_____
_____
_____
_____

http://theproductivityexperts.com/52-powerful-success-strategies/powerful-results-form

Action:

Use the 5-10-15 Rule

Ever have a project you just can't seem to get started on? Try using the following process:

- Commit to working on the project for just 5 minutes — Set a timer. When time is up you can stop or...
- Commit to 10 minutes — Again, set a timer. The first 5 minutes got you started; 10 minutes will get you further. When time is up you can stop or...
- Set the timer one more time for 15 minutes — At the end of the 15 minutes, you'll have worked focused for 30 minutes and moved your project along — or maybe even completed it.

Quote:

"The two rules of procrastination: 1) Do it today. 2) Tomorrow will be today tomorrow."
~ Author Unknown

Affirmation:

"Why can I stay focused and move my projects forward so easily?"

How does this tip, quote or afformation relate to you and your productivity?

_____

_____

_____

_____

_____

_____

_____

_____

_____

_____

What will you improve, change, STOP or start doing this week?

_____

_____

_____

_____

_____

_____

_____

_____

_____

_____

_____

http://theproductivityexperts.com/52-powerful-success-strategies/powerful-results-form

Other Resources:

What's your productivity challenge?
https://app.hatchbuck.com/OnlineForm/50165738227

Productivity self-assessment:
http://theproductivityexperts.com/self-assessment

Productivity store
http://theproductivityexperts.com/shop/

For More Weekly Actions
http://theproductivityexperts.com/tips/

25 Productivity Strategies to get more done eBook
http://theproductivityexperts.com/ebook-bonus

Productivity Blog
http://theproductivityexperts.com/blog/

Check out Cathy Sexton's speaking schedule
http://theproductivityexperts.com/productivity-speaker/
cathys-calendar/

Chapter Six

POWERFUL = Focus: Planning, Interruptions and Distractions

Are you distracted and going in too many directions?

Do you find yourself trying to focus on too many things at once?

Do you feel overwhelmed because you have too many "irons in the fire" and no clear plan for where to start?

To get more done and remain competitive and highly successful, staying focused is key. Everyone has trouble staying focused at times. Lack of planning, multiple interruptions, distractions and trying to do too many things at once can all negatively affect productivity.

Strive to have a single-purpose focus. In other words, focus on one thing at a time. As you go through your day, you will gradually see your to-do list diminishing. Stick to one thing, because once you get distracted it can be hard to get back on track. Take it one minute and one task at a time.

Each day ask yourself:

- What is the most important thing I have to do today?
- What matters the most on my schedule?

Then prioritize and focus on those things.

Action:

Reflect on the Week

Friday will be here before you know it. The week will be over and you can finally leave work behind, relax and enjoy the weekend. Wait! Before you get into full relaxation mode, why not use Friday afternoon to review your schedule from the past week and double-check what you did and didn't get done. Take your time going over your schedule. You may be tempted to quickly glance over it and get that relaxing weekend started, but making sure you completed everything vital that was on your schedule will make your weekend even more enjoyable. It gives you the opportunity to tie up any loose ends if you find something important you forgot to do — which will keep that pesky task from popping up as an emergency during your down time. It also allows you to celebrate what you did get done and experience that wonderful sense of satisfaction over the productive week you had, so you can truly enjoy the weekend.

Quote:

"There are no shortcuts to any place worth going."
~ Beverly Sills

Afformation:

"Why do I reflect on my past schedule so easily?"

How does this tip, quote or afformation relate to you and your productivity?

_____

_____

_____

_____

_____

_____

_____

_____

_____

_____

_____

What will you improve, change, STOP or start doing this week?

_____

_____

_____

_____

_____

_____

_____

_____

_____

_____

_____

_____

_____

http://theproductivityexperts.com/52-powerful-success-strategies/powerful-results-form

Action:

Maintain a Master Calendar

Work calendar, travel calendar, home calendar, church calendar, kids activity calendar, school calendar, others?

You may have heard me say this before; "You have *one life*, so you only need *one calendar*."

Keep all time commitments, whether professional, personal, or family, in a single planner or calendar. If you don't, sooner or later you will miss an appointment or over-book yourself. It doesn't matter if it's electronic or paper (truthfully, I have both). I like to carry a paper calendar with me, so I can see the whole week at a glance. At the end of the day, I sync the paper calendar with my electronic one — which then syncs (automatically) to my phone.

*Note: For scheduling meetings when I have to travel, I always add the travel time in the calendar so I know what time I have to leave.

Quote:

"We have to do the best we can. This is our sacred human responsibility."
~ Albert Einstein

Afformation:

"Why is my calendar always up to date?"

How does this tip, quote or afformation relate to you and your productivity?

_____
_____
_____
_____
_____
_____
_____
_____
_____
_____

What will you improve, change, STOP or start doing this week?

_____
_____
_____
_____
_____
_____
_____
_____
_____
_____
_____

http://theproductivityexperts.com/52-powerful-success-strategies/powerful-results-form

Action:

Prepare for Vacations

It's time to get the desk cleaned off so you can enjoy the vacation clutter free.

Sorting piles or an inbox? Sort from the top down. Don't skip around. To create and maintain order requires working in an orderly manner. Handle papers one at a time, from the top of the master pile. Resist the urge to dig out something farther down that may relate to the one in your hand. Make a decision.

- Does it need to be deleted? Delegated? Filed? Action Taken? — Just Do It or schedule for later.
- Schedule time prior to and after returning from vacation to allow time to prepare and get caught up.

Quote:

"If we are together, nothing is impossible. If we are divided, all will fail."
~ Winston Churchill

Afformation:

"Why am I always so caught up and prepared for vacation time?"

How does this tip, quote or afformation relate to you and your productivity?

_____
_____
_____
_____
_____
_____
_____
_____
_____
_____
_____

What will you improve, change, STOP or start doing this week?

_____
_____
_____
_____
_____
_____
_____
_____
_____
_____
_____
_____
_____

http://theproductivityexperts.com/52-powerful-success-strategies/powerful-results-form

Action:

Group Interruptions

Do you find yourself being interrupted frequently throughout the day? Someone may come in every 30 minutes with a different question. You can cut down on interruptions by grouping them. Ask your assistant to collect all questions or interruptions in a list, then once or twice a day you can go through them — unless it is urgent then, of course, answer it immediately. By grouping your interruptions, you and your staff can get a lot more accomplished.

Quote:

"Every choice you make has an end result."
~ Zig Ziglar

Afformation:

"Why am I receiving fewer interruptions?"

How does this tip, quote or afformation relate to you and your productivity?

_____

_____

_____

_____

_____

_____

_____

_____

_____

_____

What will you improve, change, STOP or start doing this week?

_____

_____

_____

_____

_____

_____

_____

_____

_____

_____

_____

_____

http://theproductivityexperts.com/52-powerful-success-strategies/powerful-results-form

Action:

Reduce Potential Interruptions

Do you get too many people interrupting you? Consider:
- Removing the candy jar from your desk.
- Removing the extra chair near your desk or replacing it with an uncomfortable one.
- Standing up when greeting others. Most people won't feel the urge to sit down if you keep standing.
- Asking how much time they need, scheduling it and holding them to the time.

Quote:

"Don't cry because it's over. Smile because it happened."
~ Unknown

Afformation:

"Why is it so easy to reduce interruptions?"

How does this tip, quote or afformation relate to you and your productivity?

_____

_____

_____

_____

_____

_____

_____

_____

_____

_____

_____

What will you improve, change, STOP or start doing this week?

_____

_____

_____

_____

_____

_____

_____

_____

_____

_____

_____

_____

http://theproductivityexperts.com/52-powerful-success-strategies/powerful-results-form

Action:

Get Rid of Distractions

Turn off the technology during your high-energy time. Pinpoint the time of day when you are at your best and remove all distractions. Turn off the technology for 45 - 90 minutes and focus on what really matters. Put your phone on DND (Do Not Disturb) and let the messages go to voice mail. Don't open up your email. You will be amazed at how much you get done. It seems difficult, but I know you can do it. Try it!

Quote:

"Many people seem to think that success in one area can compensate for failure in other areas. But can it really? True effectiveness requires balance."
~ Stephen Covey

Afformation:

"Why is it so easy to get rid of distractions?"

How does this tip, quote or afformation relate to you and your
productivity?

_____

_____

_____

_____

_____

_____

_____

_____

_____

_____

What will you improve, change, STOP or start doing this week?

_____

_____

_____

_____

_____

_____

_____

_____

_____

_____

_____

_____

_____

http://theproductivityexperts.com/52-powerful-success-strategies/powerful-results-form

Action:

Plan Your Goals

Are you meeting your goals? Have you thought about what the final result will look like for each goal? To help achieve your goals, start with the end in mind. Put a deadline on your goals: Next Monday, the end of January, December 31, 2016, your birthday, etc. By determining the finish date, you can then work backwards with actions steps and milestones. This way, you can see if your end date is do-able.

Quote:

"Plans are nothing; planning is everything."
~ Dwight D. Eisenhower

Afformation:

"Why do I achieve my goals on time?"

How does this tip, quote or afformation relate to you and your productivity?

_____

_____

_____

_____

_____

_____

_____

_____

_____

_____

What will you improve, change, STOP or start doing this week?

_____

_____

_____

_____

_____

_____

_____

_____

_____

_____

_____

http://theproductivityexperts.com/52-powerful-success-strategies/powerful-results-form

Action:

Plan, Plan, Then Plan Some More

Are you a planner? Or are you only thinking about the next thing that needs to be done?

Take a few minutes at the end of the week to review all your projects and deadlines for the rest of the month. This will give you time to fit project due dates into your daily/weekly to-do list. This will help eliminate the pressure and stress of the down-to-the-wire deadlines.

Quote:

"Plans are nothing; planning is everything."
~ Dwight D. Eisenhower

Afformation

"Why is it so easy to be on top of projects?"

How does this tip, quote or afformation relate to you and your productivity?

_____

_____

_____

_____

_____

_____

_____

_____

_____

_____

What will you improve, change, STOP or start doing this week?

_____

_____

_____

_____

_____

_____

_____

_____

_____

_____

_____

_____

http://theproductivityexperts.com/52-powerful-success-strategies/powerful-results-form

Other Resources:

What's your productivity challenge?
https://app.hatchbuck.com/OnlineForm/50165738227

Productivity self-assessment:
http://theproductivityexperts.com/self-assessment

Productivity store
http://theproductivityexperts.com/shop/

For More Weekly Actions
http://theproductivityexperts.com/tips/

25 Productivity Strategies to get more done eBook
http://theproductivityexperts.com/ebook-bonus

Productivity Blog
http://theproductivityexperts.com/blog/

Check out Cathy Sexton's speaking schedule
http://theproductivityexperts.com/productivity-speaker/
cathys-calendar/

Chapter Seven

POWERFUL = Utilization: Time and Energy

How we utilize our time can have a huge impact on our productivity. We tend to think of time in terms of "big chunks" that we'll devote to the tasks to be completed, but these days, when everything moves at such a fast pace, it's important to have a mindset of making every minute count.

In this chapter, you'll find tips for helping you maximize your time and make use of every minute in your workday. From creating better action lists to identifying and making the most of your peak energy time, these simple ideas will help you stay on top of what you need to do, keep it all organized in your mind and get it all done.

Action:

Create Better To-Do Lists

Many productive people make to-do lists. However, not getting specific enough can result in confusion and may even cause you to skip a to-do. You can improve your to-do lists with simple steps.

- Be more specific.
- Break up a large project into smaller tasks.
- List the next step vs. end results.
- Keep it visible — if you can't see it, you probably won't do it.
- Use reminders. The reminders can be digital or even sticky notes.
- Small steps can ensure you achieve your desired to-do list.

Quote:

"One of the secrets of getting more done is to make a To Do List every day, keep it visible, and use it as a guide to action as you go through the day."
~ Alan Lakein

Afformation:

"Why is it so easy for me to accomplish my to-do list?"

How does this tip, quote or afformation relate to you and your productivity?

_____

_____

_____

_____

_____

_____

_____

_____

_____

_____

What will you improve, change, STOP or start doing this week?

_____

_____

_____

_____

_____

_____

_____

_____

_____

_____

_____

_____

http://theproductivityexperts.com/52-powerful-success-strategies/powerful-results-form

Action:

Work From an Action List

Have a lot to do? Feeling overwhelmed? First do a "Brain Dump." Get out a piece of paper and write down everything that's floating around in your head. Write down all the: want, need, must, should, committed to, and maybe someday I'll do. *"You cannot organize or prioritize it if it's in your head."*

- Separate out *the important things* from this list that need to get done.
- Delegate anything from your list that someone else can do.
- Prioritize your tasks by due date.
- List the length of time it will take.
- Break projects into small tasks and always think of the next action.
- If the task takes more than 45 minutes, put it on your calendar.

Quote:

"A real decision is measured by the fact that you've taken a new action. If there's no action, you haven't truly decided."
~ Tony Robbins

Afformation

"Why do I always do a "Brain Dump" when I am feeling overwhelmed?"

How does this tip, quote or afformation relate to you and your productivity?

_____

_____

_____

_____

_____

_____

_____

_____

_____

_____

What will you improve, change, STOP or start doing this week?

_____

_____

_____

_____

_____

_____

_____

_____

_____

_____

_____

_____

http://theproductivityexperts.com/52-powerful-success-strategies/powerful-results-form

Action:

Distinguish Urgent vs. Important

Just because something appears urgent doesn't mean it's important. Important activities are those that help you achieve your goals and dreams. Don't let others' urgent items become your priorities. The key is to know which tasks are important for you to accomplish today, so that you can make better decisions when urgent items come up.

- Work on one project at a time (your most important of the day).
- Work from a clean desk so your project is the only item in front of you.
- When interruption comes, decide which is most important to devote your time to: the task at hand or the issue that caused the interruption.

Quote:

"Everything is perfect in the universe — even your desire to improve it."
~ Wayne Dyer

Afformation

"Why do I know my most important project and avoid other's urgencies?"

How does this tip, quote or afformation relate to you and your productivity?

_____

_____

_____

_____

_____

_____

_____

_____

_____

_____

_____

What will you improve, change, STOP or start doing this week?

_____

_____

_____

_____

_____

_____

_____

_____

_____

_____

_____

_____

_____

http://theproductivityexperts.com/52-powerful-success-strategies/powerful-results-form

Action:

Make Your Commute Productive

Do you commute to work? Perhaps you take the bus, metro, or ride with a friend. Do you ever find yourself getting bored while waiting to get to work? Why not go over your schedule for the day? Know what you will be doing and where you need to be. This is a productive way to make use of your commute time. Perhaps, you ride with friends from work. Why not go over ideas together? Prepare yourself for the day ahead of you. That way, when you get to work, you will be prepared and ready for whatever may come your way.

Quote:

"Nothing makes a person more productive than the last minute."
~ Starcharon

Afformation:

"Why am I so productive on my commute to work?"

How does this tip, quote or afformation relate to you and your productivity?

_____
_____
_____
_____
_____
_____
_____
_____
_____
_____
_____

What will you improve, change, STOP or start doing this week?

_____
_____
_____
_____
_____
_____
_____
_____
_____
_____
_____
_____

http://theproductivityexperts.com/52-powerful-success-strategies/powerful-results-form

Action:

Make Good Use of Time

Make good use of waiting time: Don't go to the doctor's office or a meeting without bringing something to do — work papers to read, industry magazines, thank you cards to catch up on, or whatever else you could be working on. Make the most of those minutes waiting on others.

Tip: For magazine articles...

> If you tear out the article from the magazine and place it in a folder, you can target your reading and have less to carry.

> Reduce the load, discard after reading.

Quote:

"A year from now you will wish you had started today."
~ Karen Lamb

Afformation:

"Why do I choose to use time wisely?"

How does this tip, quote or afformation relate to you and your productivity?

_____
_____
_____
_____
_____
_____
_____
_____
_____
_____

What will you improve, change, STOP or start doing this week?

_____
_____
_____
_____
_____
_____
_____
_____
_____
_____
_____
_____

http://theproductivityexperts.com/52-powerful-success-strategies/powerful-results-form

Action:

Find Your Peak Energy Time

When is your peak energy time: morning, noon, after lunch, afternoon, evening, or late night?

We all have different peak energy times; some of us are night owls, while others are early birds. But most people have various peak times throughout the day. It's important to know when your peak energy time is and make the most of it.

When your energy level is at its highest, tackle the most difficult projects or the ones that take the most brain energy. Don't try and do these types of tasks when your energy level is low, because it will probably take you twice as long to complete than if you did them during your peak energy level.

Quote:

"It takes a lot of courage to show your dreams to someone else."
~ Erma Bombeck

Afformation:

"Why is it so easy to take advantage of my peak energy time?"

How does this tip, quote or afformation relate to you and your productivity?

_____

_____

_____

_____

_____

_____

_____

_____

_____

_____

_____

What will you improve, change, STOP or start doing this week?

_____

_____

_____

_____

_____

_____

_____

_____

_____

_____

_____

_____

http://theproductivityexperts.com/52-powerful-success-strategies/powerful-results-form

Action:

Focus on One Change for 30 Days

First, analyze your current situation to pinpoint the areas of your life where you've been wasting or inefficiently using your time, energy, and resources. Then, choose one thing to work on for the next 30 days. Make this your focus every day for the next 30 days and see how much you get accomplished while focusing on just that one major change.

Quote:

"The one lesson I have learned in life is that there is no substitute for paying attention."
~ Diane Sawyer

Afformation:

"Why do I stay focused on one change at a time?"

How does this tip, quote or afformation relate to you and your productivity?

_____

_____

_____

_____

_____

_____

_____

_____

_____

_____

_____

What will you improve, change, STOP or start doing this week?

_____

_____

_____

_____

_____

_____

_____

_____

_____

_____

_____

_____

_____

http://theproductivityexperts.com/52-powerful-success-strategies/powerful-results-form

Action:

Take 10

Things can get hectic as we juggle all of the demands of daily activities and commitments.

Take just 10 minutes at the end of each day to recap the following things:
- All that you accomplished today. It may not have been what you planned, but you got a lot done! Enjoy that productivity.
- What needs to happen tomorrow?
- What worked today, what didn't work today, and what needs to change?

These few minutes will change the way you work and what you get accomplished, which will help you move closer to your goals.

Quote:

"One can always trust time. Insert a wedge of time and nearly everything straightens itself out."
~ Norman Douglas

Afformation:

"Why do I choose to 'take 10'?"

How does this tip, quote or afformation relate to you and your productivity?

_____

_____

_____

_____

_____

_____

_____

_____

_____

_____

What will you improve, change, STOP or start doing this week?

_____

_____

_____

_____

_____

_____

_____

_____

_____

_____

_____

_____

http://theproductivityexperts.com/52-powerful-success-strategies/powerful-results-form

Other Resources:

What's your productivity challenge?
https://app.hatchbuck.com/OnlineForm/50165738227

Productivity self-assessment:
http://theproductivityexperts.com/self-assessment

Productivity store
http://theproductivityexperts.com/shop/

For More Weekly Actions
http://theproductivityexperts.com/tips/

25 Productivity Strategies to get more done eBook
http://theproductivityexperts.com/ebook-bonus

Productivity Blog
http://theproductivityexperts.com/blog/

Check out Cathy Sexton's speaking schedule
http://theproductivityexperts.com/productivity-speaker/
cathys-calendar/

Chapter Eight

POWERFUL = Leverage Resources: Technology and Delegation

We are fortunate to live in a time when we have more resources to help us be productive than ever before. It's true, technology creates challenges, but it also gives us the ability to get things done faster and easier. We can communicate quickly and efficiently with clients and co-workers, share project documents in Dropbox, organize tasks in a central calendar so all team members can see current projects and deadlines and send an email instead of snail-mail or playing phone tag. The list could go on and on.

Learning to effectively leverage technology, staff, and other resources available to us is a great way to boost our productivity and make the best use of our time.

Action:

Ask the Right Questions

Ask yourself:

"Why am I doing what I'm doing right now?" — and ask it often. Always evaluate what you're doing to make sure that you're making the most productive use of your time and moving in the direction of your goals.

"Can someone else be doing this?" Delegate, Delegate, Delegate.

"Is what I'm doing... making money, retaining/creating clients, contributing to the bottom line, etc.?"

Quote:

"Genius is one percent inspiration and ninety-nine percent perspiration."
~ Thomas A. Edison

Afformation:

"Why do I always ask the right questions?"

How does this tip, quote or afformation relate to you and your productivity?

_____

_____

_____

_____

_____

_____

_____

_____

_____

_____

What will you improve, change, STOP or start doing this week?

_____

_____

_____

_____

_____

_____

_____

_____

_____

_____

_____

_____

http://theproductivityexperts.com/52-powerful-success-strategies/powerful-results-form

Action:

Delegate the To-Do List

I've said it before and I'll say it again: one of the best tools to use to get it all done... Delegate.

Just because it needs to be done does not mean YOU have to do it. If you can delegate most of your list and only do what you're good at or enjoy doing, a lot more will get done.

For every item on your to-do list, ask yourself the following key questions:
- Can someone else do it?
- Is this the best use of my time?
- Is this going to help me reach my goals?
- Will I do it? Does it really need to be done or is it just something on my list?

Quote:

"No man goes before his time — unless the boss leaves early."
~ Groucho Marx

Afformation:

"Why am I so good at delegating?"

How does this tip, quote or afformation relate to you and your productivity?

_____

_____

_____

_____

_____

_____

_____

_____

_____

_____

_____

What will you improve, change, STOP or start doing this week?

_____

_____

_____

_____

_____

_____

_____

_____

_____

_____

_____

_____

http://theproductivityexperts.com/52-powerful-success-strategies/powerful-results-form

Action:

Be Prepared for the Dreaded Computer Crash

Have you ever had to upgrade your computer or reinstall software after a crash and end up searching and searching for the product installation key codes?

We all know we should keep all our documentation, but sometimes that just doesn't happen. Even if we do keep it, it's easy to forget where we even put that information after long periods of time. Here are two suggestions to make it easier next time.

- Use a sharpie marker and write the product key right on the CD. Then you just have to remember where you put the CD. Buy a storage container to keep all software CDs and manuals/instructions in one place. The small investment in a storage container could save you time and frustration if you ever need that information.
- Using Outlook? Use your notes in Outlook and create a note for software license keys and product codes — this is also a great place to track support phone numbers or keep information in a spreadsheet.

Why not do both?

Quote:

"Worry is like a rocking chair: it gives you something to do but never gets you anywhere."
~ Erma Bombeck

Afformation:

"Why do I always have the right information at my fingertips?

How does this tip, quote or afformation relate to you and your productivity?

_____

_____

_____

_____

_____

_____

_____

_____

_____

_____

_____

What will you improve, change, STOP or start doing this week?

_____

_____

_____

_____

_____

_____

_____

_____

_____

_____

_____

_____

http://theproductivityexperts.com/52-powerful-success-strategies/powerful-results-form

Action:

Capture Creativity

Have a project coming up, but you're struggling with a creativity block? Do you have a creative staff? Hold a team meeting and ask for ideas. You will most likely realize that there are a lot of creative members on your team. You might even be amazed by how many ideas you come up with by utilizing collaborative brainstorming. Asking for ideas is also a way to let everyone have a chance to voice their ideas and contribute to the success of a project. Let someone know when he or she has a really good idea. It will boost their self-confidence and overall team morale by knowing that you listen to their ideas. Capture all that untapped creativity and see what you can come up with.

Quote:

"Creativity is intelligence having fun."
~ Albert Einstein

Afformation:

"How was it so easy to spark creativity?"

How does this tip, quote or afformation relate to you and your productivity?

_____

_____

_____

_____

_____

_____

_____

_____

_____

_____

What will you improve, change, STOP or start doing this week?

_____

_____

_____

_____

_____

_____

_____

_____

_____

_____

_____

http://theproductivityexperts.com/52-powerful-success-strategies/powerful-results-form

Action:

Share Files Efficiently

Do you ever need to share files with someone? Do you need to keep files in one place where you or others can work on them and not have a million different versions? Dropbox, One Drive, Google Drive, etc. are free services that allow you to put files in a folder and share that folder with others. Using these tools to share files to work with virtual assistants, co-workers, team members, committee members, etc. will save time, frustration, and sanity. Try it out, and let me know if it works for you.

Remember, the service is free and you'll always have your stuff when you need it or to share it.

Quote:

"The only time you run out of chances is when you stop taking them."
~ Unknown

Afformation:

"Why do I choose to use Dropbox or other file sharing programs?"

How does this tip, quote or afformation relate to you and your productivity?

_____

_____

_____

_____

_____

_____

_____

_____

_____

_____

What will you improve, change, STOP or start doing this week?

_____

_____

_____

_____

_____

_____

_____

_____

_____

_____

_____

_____

http://theproductivityexperts.com/52-powerful-success-strategies/powerful-results-form

Action:

Know When to Delegate

When working towards your goals, it's all about the activities and deciding whether or not certain activities are the best use of your time, or if someone else could/should be doing it. So is it time to let others help you with certain activities? By not delegating, you are placing a heavy burden on yourself, which can cause stress and being overwhelmed. Start thinking delegation. The right time to delegate a job is when you face any of these tasks:

- Routine
- Technical
- Short
- Those you don't have time for
- Those that train others
- Those you dread doing

Quote:

"Life is a great big canvas; throw all the paint on it you can."
~ Danny Kaye

Afformation:

"Why do I choose to delegate?"

How does this tip, quote or afformation relate to you and your productivity?

_____

_____

_____

_____

_____

_____

_____

_____

_____

_____

_____

What will you improve, change, STOP or start doing this week?

_____

_____

_____

_____

_____

_____

_____

_____

_____

_____

_____

_____

http://theproductivityexperts.com/52-powerful-success-strategies/powerful-results-form

Other Resources:

What's your productivity challenge?
https://app.hatchbuck.com/OnlineForm/50165738227

Productivity self-assessment:
http://theproductivityexperts.com/self-assessment

Productivity store
http://theproductivityexperts.com/shop/

For More Weekly Actions
http://theproductivityexperts.com/tips/

25 Productivity Strategies to get more done eBook
http://theproductivityexperts.com/ebook-bonus

Productivity Blog
http://theproductivityexperts.com/blog/

Check out Cathy Sexton's speaking schedule
http://theproductivityexperts.com/productivity-speaker/
cathys-calendar/

Find these, along with other productivity resources at
http://theproductivityexperts.com/shop/

Daily T.I.P.s — Note Pad/Mouse Pad — Stay on top of your Top Important Priorities

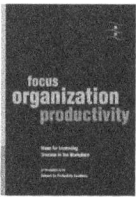

"Focus. Organization. Productivity." — A collection of simple ideas written by members of the Network for Productivity Excellence — including Cathy Sexton

"Exploring Productivity" — A collection of ideas written by members of the Network for Productivity Excellence — including Cathy Sexton

"7 Points of Impact" — A collection of inspirational, motivational, heartfelt and thought-provoking perspectives from 52 Personal Coaches, Peer Advocates, Business Mentors and Spiritual Teachers — including Cathy Sexton

Conclusion

Thank you for reading *52 POWERFUL Strategies to Ignite Your Productivity* and sharing this journey with me. I realize you may have heard a lot of these tips before and even tried to implement them, but sometimes just the timing and the way it's stated or explained makes all the difference in our understanding and willingness to make changes. Sadly, even once we're willing to change, most will not implement the changes long enough for them to take hold. Don't allow yourself to get discouraged. Remember, each new day offers us the opportunity to try again and be better. Change is a process, not a one-time event.

When thinking about changing habits or routines, there's no better time to start than today. Take time to think through the pros and cons of your current situation and what really needs to change. It's much easier to modify something you're already doing than to do a 180, though at times the 180 is necessary. Start slow and implement small changes at a time. It is truly about finding out what works for you. It's not about what you think you **should** do, it's about what you **can and will** do.

There is always something more to learn and another challenge to conquer. My greatest hope is that you found these tips helpful, were inspired to implement them to ignite your productivity, and that you continue to actively work toward elevating your productivity and making a positive difference in your life and the lives of those around you.

Cathy Sexton
Productivity & Profit First Specialist
The Productivity Experts
Cathy@TheProductivityExperts.com
314-267-3969
www.TheProductivityExperts.com

About the Author

Productivity and Profit First Specialist, Speaker, Author and Coach, Cathy Sexton helps individuals and organizations I.G.N.I.T.E. Productivity and Increase Profits. Delivering high-impact principles through speaking, coaching, training and special resources, Cathy empowers people to achieve their life and business goals, make the profit they desire and still have time for family and friends.

Cathy founded The Productivity Experts in 2003 after winning her own battle with workaholism and a stress-induced, life-threatening illness. Cathy is committed to helping people accomplish more, with less stress. Professionals can now avoid burnout, spend more quality time with their family and make the money they deserve.

Cathy's easy processes are taught through 1-on-1 and group coaching, seminars, workshops and her unique "I.G.N.I.T.E.™" and "Productivity to Profit™" programs. Attendees and participants learn how to take control of their thoughts, processes and tools to achieve better results, faster.

Cathy is the author of *52 POWERFUL Success Strategies to Ignite Productivity* and co-author of *Focus, Organization and Productivity, Exploring Productivity* and *7 Points of Impact*.